The ABCs of Money:

Always

Be mindful of

Christ!

Karen N. Tobias

The ABCs of Money: Always Be mindful of Christ!

ISBN: 0-7392-0308-8

Library of Congress Catalog Card Number: 99-94999

Printed in the USA by

MP
MORRIS PUBLISHING

3212 East Highway 30 • Kearney, NE 68847 • 1-800-650-7888

Dedication

This book is especially dedicated to my grandmother,
Rosie Lee May.

Acknowledgments

One thing I have learned, especially in writing this book, is that accomplishing anything in life requires the help of those around you. Because of this knowledge, I strongly believe that when people do nice things for you, it is always polite to let them know how much you appreciate their time and support. So, I want to take this time to thank the people who helped this book come into existence.

To God:
Your name is worthy to be praised!
Thank you Lord! Thank you Lord!
Hallelujah! Hallelujah! Thank you Lord!

To Mom & Dad:
Thanks for your support and guidance
and for teaching me the ABCs of life.
Even in this, I must Always Be mindful of Christ.
I love you!

To Sir Rod:
Thanks for always looking out for your big sister.
I love you and stay strong, my brother!

To my two church families,
Neshoba & Joy Apostolic Church - Pastor Genoria Tobias
and
Mt. Moriah Holiness Church - Pastor James Robinson:
I give thanks to God for allowing me two church families,
whom I love dearly. Mercy unto you,
and peace, and love, be multiplied!

To a special church family,
Full Gospel Tabernacle - Pastor Wayne Lacy:
I KNOW YOU'VE GOT MY BACK!

To the "Five Friends"
Nicole, Faith, Sylvia, Trish and Wanda:
Thank you for allowing me to be your friend.
Abundant blessings always.

To the Women's Outreach Alliance Ministry:
It was with you that I conducted
my first seminar on being debt free.
From the bottom of my heart, I thank you.

To the "special helpers"
Anita, Rebecca, Debbie, Sandra, Cassius, Ira, and Eddie:
Thanks for making sure I have my ABCs in the right place,
and also for your words of encouragement.
I pray that God gives you special blessings!

I also want to say a big thank you to all of the churches that
allowed me to come in and spread the good news of God's
financial plan. There are many others I would like to thank, but I
wouldn't have enough room to write the book, so let it be known
that I thank all of you . . . and especially you. Keep me in your
prayers and you will constantly be in mine.

Remember to Always Be mindful of Christ!

Contents

Dedication 3
Acknowledgments 4
Introduction 9

My Testimony 11

Part I: The Foundation

One: Steward Defined 19
Two: It's Not Enough to Just be a Steward 21
Three: Do You Have the Right Attitude? 22
Four: Are You in Financial Bondage? 24
Five: Priorities: First Things First 26
Six: The First Part Belongs to God! 27
Seven: Give, Give, Give 29
Eight: Things vs. Money 31
Nine: Success From God's Perspective 33
Ten: Finding Contentment 35

Part II: Financial Planning - God's Way

Eleven: Got a Plan? 41
Twelve: Balance Your Checkbook 46
Thirteen: Develop a Spending Plan 48
Fourteen: Reduce or Eliminate the Use of Credit 51
Fifteen: Know What's on Your Credit Report 56
Sixteen: Start a Savings Plan 58
Seventeen: Using Wisdom When It Comes to Spending 60
Eighteen: What About Bankruptcy? 63

A Final Word 66
References 67

Introduction

Praise God from whom all blessings flow! First, I want to thank and give all honor to God, because without Him bestowing upon me His abundant blessings, I would not be where I am today. I could begin listing all of those blessings, but I only want to focus on one area - finances. God has blessed me to become debt free and I want to give my testimony and a few tips on how you, too, can achieve financial freedom.

In saying that, let me begin by saying that this will not be a book about investing in the stock market nor will it be about how to get your hands on big bucks quickly. Nope. This book will focus on God's Money 101. The basics. You can't be an investor if you have nothing to invest. And why should God give you more money if you can't manage what you have now? Many people share the idea that more money will solve all the problems that they may be facing. This idea is warped especially if you can't let God rule your life and your finances.

It is my prayer that in reading this book, you will see that financial freedom can be achieved, but only if you are willing to Always Be mindful of Christ!

MY TESTIMONY

The fear of the Lord is the beginning of wisdom:
and the knowledge of the holy is understanding.
Proverbs 9:10

Carrying debt . . . (pant, pant) . . . too long . . .
(pant, pant) . . .debt is heavy . . . (pant, pant) . . .
Must repent! Hear my cry, O Lord!

Getting into debt is quite easy. All it takes is a willingness to believe that you can afford anything you want, as long as you make low monthly payments until the bill is paid in full. Everyone makes it sound so simple. Can't afford to pay cash up front to get a car? Get a loan. Can't afford to pay cash up front for a home? Get a loan. Loans can be fairly easy to get; however, no one tells you about what happens when you don't realize the full consequences of your actions. But don't get ahead of me. Loans are not bad things to have. Loans can be very helpful in acquiring the things you need. What I need for you to understand is that not having a game plan in place for repaying the debt, in the least amount of time, can make things more complicated in the long run.

I started accumulating debt beginning with my first year in college. Because scholarships didn't cover all of my expenses, my only other option was to get a student loan. Because I didn't need to have a cosigner, it was all up to me to pay back every last dime once my college education was completed. Whereas another person may have just brushed this off and thought about it later, I couldn't just let it slide. I became very aware of the fact that I - yes, I - was paying my way through school. From the moment I signed my name on the dotted line, I made a promise to be a good student, learn what I could, and get the best grades possible. If I was going to have to pay, then I wanted something to show for it.

Because I didn't want to solely rely on student loans to help me through school, I found employment opportunities on campus and I also worked during the summers to obtain extra cash. Because cash was always a little short when the school year began, (and why do books have to cost so much anyway?) I fell victim to a common trap laid to college students - the *credit card application*! I applied for one thinking that I could always keep a handle on my expenditures and for a while I did. But then unexpected things would arise and I wouldn't have enough cash on hand to handle the situation. Forget about asking God what to do and waiting for an answer. I needed the money now and I would worry about how to make the payments on my credit card later. Fortunately, I was able to tame my spending habits and by the time I graduated college in 1992, after five long years, the only debt I had was the student loan.

Now here comes the good part. I didn't get into the debt trap until 1994. I had just acquired a new car and moved into a new apartment when the most amazing thing happened. I had to quit my job. I found that I really didn't have enough in savings to help me, so I started looking for temporary work until something permanent came along. I began to realize, after a period of time, that working for the temporary service wasn't going to cut it. My debts and expenses were much more than my income. I began to do unheard of things like using my credit card more, juggling bills just to stay afloat and not asking God for help. Thank God for the prayers of the righteous, because I was a traveler without a road map and I needed help. Bills were accumulating and no one seemed to be offering permanent employment. Satan began to play with my mind and tell me things like, "I thought Jesus loved you. If He loved you, why are you suffering? Why would He allow you to leave a job and not give you another one? Why doesn't He send you any help? If you would only listen to me, I could show you many ways to help you get back on your feet in a hurry." To be honest, sometimes I listened. I didn't listen for long though. I had a problem that needed to be fixed.

After about four months of being frustrated and feeling out of control, I decided something needed to be done. You'll never believe what I did! I got on my knees and began to pray. (The nerve of me, right?) I started first by repenting to God for not allowing Him to do what He had been waiting to do all the time – guide me. God was putting me to the test and I was failing miserably. I had to come to the conclusion that I was responsible for my problems, and even though I proclaimed to love the Lord, I did not allow him into the one area of my life where He needed to be the most – my money. He wanted me to trust Him in everything but yet I thought I could handle the money aspect all by myself.

You know, it's an amazing thing when you take your burdens to the Lord and allow Him to do His thing. I was still working, via temporary employment services, but the biggest difference was the change in my attitude. It was time to put on my armor and fight! The Lord had already proclaimed that I would be victorious and now Satan had to be put in his place. To show the Lord I believed what He said, I had to step out on faith and walk in the right direction. I began to search God's Word (The Bible) in order to find out what God had to say about His money. Then I asked the Lord to give me a job but not just any job. I wanted a job that would allow me to do what I liked doing and pay me enough money to get out of the debt that I had accumulated. How much debt had I accumulated? Would you believe that I didn't know? I had an idea but now it was time to get specific. I had to take the blinders off. Putting pen to paper, I figured my total amount of debt. I owed close to $20,000 (this amount included school loans, a car loan, and credit card debt)! By going to the library and reading various books, I began to develop a budget that would allow me to see what needed to be fixed, and how much income I would need to have in order to fix it. I also found books on ways to help me deal with creditors, and books on how to understand the fine print of credit cards.

By October 1994, I was permanently employed, in the type of job I wanted, and making good money. The Lord had given me what I asked for and now it was my turn to step out on faith again. I needed someone that could help me to consolidate the debts I had, and allow me to make one payment a month verses five or six. In December 1994, I met Cathy, one of the counselors at Consumer Counseling Credit Service (CCCS), and she helped me to get my debts consolidated. All I had to do was make the scheduled payments to CCCS on my paydays and they would take care of the rest. It took some time but by March 1998, I was debt free! I had put God first and He gave me the desires of my heart! The shackles of debt had been removed and I had emerged victorious!

I want to encourage you to use your bibles, along with reading this book, in order to help you understand what is being written. You need to know **for yourself** what God's Word has in it, because now that you want to do what's right, Satan is right there waiting to see how he can get you to turn your back on the truth. Many of God's children are suffering because of a lack of knowledge. Satan has taken the very riches, provided by God to enrich our lives and bring others to salvation, and has diverted them for his use. Take a good look around you. Many Christians evaluate others on the basis of how much they have and how successful they are in worldly terms. The poor are thought to be losers - less spiritual than the winners. So guess what it's time for us as Christians to do? It's time to educate ourselves on the basics of money. The best way to defeat Satan is to learn his tricks and show him up to be the liar that he is. Being in debt is being in bondage. Believe me, I know.

Are you ready to begin? Well, let's get started. Read on!

PART I

THE FOUNDATION

And ye shall know the truth, and the truth shall make you free.
John 8:32

| ESTABLISH SURPLUS |
| PAY DEBTS |
| TAKE CARE OF FAMILY NEEDS |
| PAY TAXES |
| PAY TITHES |

Ok, stewards! Welcome to basic training! We are going to start from the bottom and work our way up. If you have any questions, feel free to ask. I'm here to help you.

Chapter One

Steward Defined

B efore you can begin handling money God's way, you need to understand your role in the matter. First of all, you have to realize who is in charge. *The earth is the Lord's and the fullness thereof: the world, and they that dwell therein - Psalm 24:1.* Everything, and I mean everything belongs to God, including the money you have.

So now you may ask, "If God is in charge, what does that make me?" You are the steward. And just what is a steward? A steward is one who manages (or who is in charge, responsible for) someone else's property. You're the babysitter and your job is to be dependable, trustworthy, and dependent upon God for the proper direction. Being a steward is not a man thing or a woman thing. It's a requirement of being a child of God. Period.

The following diagram represents the financial life of many people:

God   > > > >   You   Money

Notice anything interesting? You are standing in the way of your own blessing! Why are you trying to keep Christ out of your financial life? Are you afraid that He doesn't know what He's doing? Do you think that you could do a better job? Remember you are a steward and as such, your financial life should look like the following diagram:

God   > > > > > > > > > > > > > > > >   Money

You

Once you move yourself out of the way and let God do His thing, you will find that God will direct you in how to handle His money. After all, it is His money and who else can beat Him as the head of your financial life? *Trust in the Lord with all thine heart; and lean not unto thine own understanding. In all thy ways acknowledge him, and he shall direct thy paths - Proverbs 3:5-6.* A side benefit will be a peace of mind because you have put God first. *When thou liest down, thou shalt not be afraid: yea, thou shalt lie down, and thy sleep shall be sweet - Proverbs 3:24.* God can choose to give us as much or as little as He desires, but in no case will we ever take ownership. Think about it, why would He entrust more property to one who began to get greedy and feel that he was the owner? If you are a Christian, then you understand that you belong to God - you are His child. If you don't know this, then here's the first step in the process: Jesus died for you. He paid the price for your sin, and He offers you eternal life with Him - if you will just accept His gift and ask Him to forgive you. This is the beginning of a new you and a new life. So, you know that you belong to God. "But," you ask, "what's this about all my stuff belonging to Him? I paid for it!"

Our entire world is one big lifetime gift to us from God. He is letting us look after His things. God has given us everything we need, from the air we breathe to the house we live in. It is our job to take care of the things God has given us, from the people we love to the little things we use every day to make our lives easier. Whether they seem important or not, they are all God's gifts.

Being a good steward can, at first, sound overwhelming. Relax! Take a deep breath. God teaches and helps us in a way that is everything but overwhelming. God set up this whole system of stewardship, not to make it harder on us, but better for us. If you do things God's way, follow His instruction manual, and trust Him to take care of you, your life will work out better.

Chapter Two

It's Not Enough to Just Be a Steward

No more beating around the bush. I've got to mention the dreaded "r" word – responsible. Why is it that no one wants to be responsible anymore? I can tell you why. It's easier to just simply shift the blame of what goes wrong on somebody else. Well, no more. Part of being a good steward is learning responsibility. This means being held accountable for your actions. Stop blaming the creditors because they call your home asking for their money. Who was bold enough to run up a bill that high in the first place? Unless someone has fraudulently used your name without your permission, I'm afraid you have no one but yourself to blame. Be bold enough to admit that you have gone in the wrong direction for too long and you want to do what's right. God wants to help you but He's not going to force Himself on you. You have to make the first step. Don't let pride get in the way. Become responsible, and you will be wonderfully surprised when you learn that God has been waiting on you. He is ready to lead you if you are willing to follow.

Chapter Three

Do You Have the Right Attitude?

L et's define attitude. Attitude is a body posture and/or behavior showing a mental state or mood. It's like a chameleon in that it changes in response to things that are happening around it. Get this inside your head: Attitude - what you do and how you act - says a lot about you! When you don't handle God's money the way that you should, the results show up in your attitude. Think back to the last time you were in church and it was time for the offering. Did the people around you seem happy to get a chance to give? Did you?

Remember the parable of the farmer in Luke 12:16-20? The farmer did wonderfully in getting and accumulating the wealth, but he messed up when he didn't consult God on how much to keep and how much to give. The farmer began to have the attitude that "I got mine, you get yours the best way you can." It is important that you do not develop this type of attitude. Remember you are dealing with God's money and He should be the ultimate manager of your money.

Above everything else, God is concerned with our attitude. The abundance or lack of money does not affect our relationship to Him - only our attitude does. Developing the right attitude can make a world of difference in becoming a financially responsible steward. For many of us, the reason we are still in a money crisis is because our attitude is all wrong. Some of us don't want God anywhere near our money telling us how to manage it properly. It's time now to unlearn bad behaviors and learn about God's teachings on a stewardship attitude:

"Everything belongs to God" attitude - Use your money with wisdom and develop an ear to hear God's voice. *Now therefore, if ye will obey my voice indeed, and keep my covenant, then ye shall be a peculiar treasure unto me above all people: for all the earth is mine - Exodus 19:5.*

"I will learn to be content" attitude - Be thankful for the things you have. *Not that I speak in respect of want: for I have learned, in whatsoever state I am, therewith to be content - Philippians 4:11.*

"I will work hard" attitude - Be willing to work and save for the things you need. *He that tilleth his land shall be satisfied with bread: but he that followeth vain persons is void of understanding - Proverbs 12:11.*

"I will learn to plan" attitude - God wants planners. *Let all things be done decently and in order - I Corinthians 14:40.*

And just how do you develop the right attitude?

Start by turning everything over to God. I beseech you therefore, brethren, by the mercies of God, that ye present your bodies a living sacrifice, holy, acceptable unto God, which is your reasonable service. And be not conformed to this world: but be ye transformed by the renewing of your mind, that ye may prove what is that good, and acceptable, and perfect, will of God - Romans 12:1-2.

Find God's plan for YOUR life. I can't be you and you can't be me. We are all unique. It would be an awful situation if everyone was destined to be a talker because who would be left to listen? Find out what God wants for you and walk therein. (Jeremiah 29:11-14; I Corinthians 15:58)

Develop a long-range viewpoint. Since God's time is not our time, it is important that we learn what patience is -- waiting. Just because you don't understand what is going on in your life, don't begin to doubt God's direction. (Matthew 6:34)

Pray without ceasing. I have often heard that prayer is God's secret weapon. Since we know that prayer is the key to unlocking God's blessings and power, let's kick the door down and begin to exercise the most powerful tool that God has given us. (I Thessalonians 5:17)

Chapter Four

Are You in Financial Bondage?

Bondage defined means captivity, being subject to a controlling person or force, a condition in which one lacks liberty to determine his or her course of action or way of life. In other words, something or someone controls you and has the power to make your life miserable. Think of bondage as being in prison. In earlier times, if a man could not pay his debts, he was thrown into debtors' prison, and his family then belonged to the lender. This bondage, physical bondage, no longer exists, but it has been replaced by another that is equally bad – financial mental bondage. Thousands of people each year are destroyed by worries caused by financial pressures. Why? Because they have violated one or more scriptural principles. So how can you tell if you're in bondage?

You are in financial bondage if you answer yes to any of the following questions:

1. Do you have overdue bills? (Read Proverbs 3:27-28)
2. Do you constantly find yourself wanting more than what you have? (Read Proverbs 30:7-9; Job 21:11-17)
3. Are you jealous of what you think others have? (Read Psalm 73:2-3; Hebrews 13:5)
4. Are you blaming others for your financial situation? (Read Proverbs 19:20-24; Philippians 2:12-15)
5. Would you rather live off others than to actually work for what you want? (Read 2 Thessalonians 3:10-12)
6. Are you working so much that your family needs are unmet? (Read I Timothy 5:8; Proverbs 23:4-5, 17-18)
7. Is work always your excuse for not having time for God? (Read Matthew 6:24-33; Psalm 127:1-2; Luke 10:38-42)
8. Are you juggling bills to keep yourself afloat? (Read 2 Peter 2:20-21; Galatians 5:1; Luke 20:20-26)

Did you see yourself in any of these situations? It's not too late to change! Today you can be financially free! Ask God right now to help you get on the right road. He's been waiting on you! St. John 8:36 reads *If the Son therefore shall make you free, ye shall be free indeed.*

Chapter Five

Priorities: First Things First!

A priority is something that should have your attention before other things. We have priorities for a reason. They help us organize our lives and understand what's important. Let's take a look at money priorities. We have a hundred things in our lives - more and more as we get older - that demand money, including our tithe, bills, food, education, and clothes. Sometimes we feel there just isn't enough money for everything. We might forget what God's purpose for money is. We might even do something that we know isn't God's way because it makes more money for us. Stop! People get caught in a lifelong trap when they put aside their Christian values for the love of money. When we use money the way God wants, we won't want for anything.

The Bible makes it very clear where God should be on our list - the top! *Thou shalt have no other gods before me - Exodus 20:3.* Your list for time and money should be God, family, friends, school or work, recreation . . . does your priority list follow God's plan for your life? It should! God has designed our lives to have balance in all things. *To every thing there is a season, and a time to every purpose under the heaven - Ecclesiastes 3:1.*

Do you feel like you have too many priorities? Are you juggling things as fast as you can? God doesn't want us to be a juggling act. Stop, get your balance, and hand off those priorities by praying to God and then give yourself a break by leaving the solution to God. *Casting all your care upon him: for he careth for you - I Peter 5:7.* When you make room for God, He'll make room for everything else.

Chapter Six

The First Part Belongs to God!

*And all the tithe of the land, whether of the seed of the land,
or of the fruit of the tree, is the Lord's: it is holy unto the Lord.
And if a man will at all redeem aught of his tithes, he shall add
thereto the fifth part thereof. And concerning the tithe of the
herd, or of the flock, even of whatsoever passeth under the rod,
the tenth shall be holy unto the Lord. He shall not search
whether it be good or bad, neither shall he change it: and if he
change it at all, then both it and the change thereof shall be holy;
it shall not be redeemed - Leviticus 27:30-33.*

I f you read Genesis 14:14-20 and Genesis 28:10-22, you
will find that tithing was practiced by Abram and Jacob
before the Old Testament law was established. Both men,
through their actions, showed that true tithing comes from a
desire to bless and please God. It also showed an understanding
that everything they had belonged to God in the first place.

Tithing is not just an Old Testament law without any real
relevance today. Because God's will and instructions for the tithe
were already well-outlined in the Old Testament, Jesus had
nothing to add to the principle except the spiritual motive of love
towards God and man, without which, giving is meaningless.
(Matthew 23:23) If the tithe belonged to God and was holy to
God then, how do you think it is any different now? Scripture
reveals in Matthew 5:17, *Think not that I am come to destroy the
law, or the prophets: I am not come to destroy, but to fulfill.*
(Also ref. Romans 10:4)

Tithe comes from the Greek word "dekate" which means part,
or tenth. Tithing is really an act of worship and should be done
with an attitude of thanksgiving. Where should you bring your
tithes? The Bible instructs to *"bring ye all the tithes into the
storehouse"* (Malachi 3:10). The storehouse is the church.

Once the tithes have been received by the church, the needs of the church can be met and the ministry of Christ can continue to move forward.

In order to tithe properly, you must give ten percent of your gross income. Why from gross income? Proverbs 3:9 reads *Honor the Lord with thy substance and with the firstfruits of all thine increase.* "Firstfruits of all thine increase" means the income before anything else is taken out. Because we are acknowledging that God is first in our lives, it is only right to give Him the first part of our income. Giving anything less than ten percent is merely an offering and you still must tithe. Even though God says in His Word that He will bless you because of your tithing (Mal 3:10b), your motivation to tithe should not be to get a blessing from God. You should tithe because God said so and because you want to increase your faith and increase God's kingdom.

After you have given tithes, it is just as important to give offerings. Not giving God tithes AND offerings makes you a thief and God warns that you will be cursed. (Malachi 3:8-9) Offerings are the amounts that are given above the tenth. Giving offerings should be even more of a joy to do because you have a chance to show God how much you really love Him.

It is sad to say but many Christians aren't tithing or aren't tithing as they should. Some of the reasons could be that many have not matured in their walk with God, or some don't have their priorities straight, or maybe it is just that they love their money more than they want to obey God. Don't let what others do keep you from doing as you should. Tithing shows that we recognize Jesus as Lord of our lives and tithing also develops our faith. If you are not presently a tither, you should begin now to become one. If you have not been tithing like you should, repent and start today doing what you now know is right. (John 13:17, James 1:25) For those of you who don't earn wages, you aren't exempt. You can still tithe! Tithing not only applies to the money you earn but it also applies to the giving of your time and talents.

Chapter Seven

Give, Give, Give

Give, and it shall be given unto you; good measure; pressed down, and shaken together, and running over, shall men give into your bosom. For with the same measure that ye mete withal it shall be measured to you again - Luke 6:38.

L earning to be a giver is probably the most important habit you can learn in your quest to become financially responsible. Let me make this one thing perfectly clear: Don't give to get! What could be more manipulative than giving ten bucks on Sunday because you desperately want a hundred on Friday? Giving back to God a portion of what He's given to us is an act of worship, gratitude, and obedience. It's always been that way as it always will be. Anything more than a no-strings-attached, no-expectations manner of giving is manipulation pure and simple.

God wants His children to be involved with the needs of others. *And the King shall answer and say unto them, Verily I say unto you, Inasmuch as ye have done it unto one of the least of these my brethren, ye have done it unto me - Matthew 25:40.* There is no better way to appreciate what we have than to observe those who truly have needs.

Would you be surprised to find that God specifically directs us not to help someone? God corrects some people by allowing them to experience material difficulties. Maybe these people need to be spiritually strengthened or maybe they have lost sight of God's will. For us to interfere is to presume His will. Some people who want help are asking for wants or desires rather than needs. We can choose to help, but we are not required to. Many people who ask for money actually need help in managing what they already have. Know that while there are many legitimate needs that warrant our gifts, there are many phonies who prefer to live off others. Don't be fooled. God warns us to be wise - "don't help those who won't help themselves. Help those who can't help themselves." (2 Thessalonians 3:10-15)

Do you have a secret problem with greed? Give. Is it tough to make the money last as long as the month? Give. Are you fearful of the future - afraid you will run out of resources, financial or otherwise? Give. When you are the neediest is when you should give the most. If giving doesn't immediately produce a burst of joy, don't worry and don't stop. Remember it's easier to act your way into a feeling than to feel your way into an action. Ask God to make you a cheerful giver.

Chapter Eight

Things vs. Money:
Which is more important to you?

Would it surprise you to learn that many people value things over money? Are you one of these people? Let me pause right now to ask a simple question: Would you like to have more money? Of course you are going to say yes. I'm sure right now if someone offered you several thousand dollars with no strings attached, you would accept it graciously. I would too. But really think about your answer. You say that you would like to have more money but how many things do you have right now that you don't even use? Some of us have five or six cars and we live alone. Who is driving all of these cars? Some of us have suits in our closet, that practically jumped into our hands at the store, but when was the first time you wore it and it's been three years since the purchase? If you want to have more money, then you have to do a better job of managing what you already have.

Picture it, you walk into a store and you see this wonderful product that you would like to purchase. A salesman approaches you and asks if he can be of service. You ask him to tell you more about this product and he explains to you the features and the cost. Now you begin to think in your head that the cost is a bit high so maybe you won't purchase this product today. The salesman sees the hesitation in your posture and quickly throws in the sales pitch that you can take this product home today, if you qualify for the installment payment plan. For low monthly payments, you can own this product and take it home today. While the salesman has left to check your credit, you think of all the fun that you are going to have once you get home and examine what you've just purchased. After a few minutes have passed, the salesman returns and tells you that you qualify for the payment plan. Without hesitation, you tell the salesman to ring up the purchase and then a contract is signed. If you had really read the contract before you signed, you would have found out that you were going to pay double what the product is worth, but right now that doesn't concern you. You've got the product you've always wanted! And besides, the salesman told you everything you needed to know.

Ask yourself the following questions:
Was this a wise purchase? Why?
Was it wrong to want the product?
What was missing in deciding to purchase the product?
Was the salesman wrong to make the sales pitch?

Christ never said money or material things were problems. He said that they were symptoms of the real problems. He constantly warns us to guard our hearts against greed, covetousness, ego, and pride, because these are the tools that Satan uses to control and manipulate this world. Now take a moment to think. Why would Christ give you this information about Satan? To prepare yourself! And just how do you do that? Learning to "pray before purchase" is your best financial weapon. Think on Matthew 6:32b-34, . . . *for your heavenly Father knoweth that ye have need of all these things. But seek ye first the kingdom of God, and his righteousness; and all these things shall be added unto you. Take therefore no thought for the morrow; for the morrow shall take thought for the things of itself. Sufficient unto the day is the evil thereof.*

Success From God's Perspective

There is nothing wrong with wanting to be successful. However, you don't want success if God isn't in the plan. Being able to have peace of mind outweighs any dollar amount that man may dangle in front of you. Success is all the sweeter when you know that you have accomplished it through God's plan. A study in God's Word reveals that material blessings were given because God loved His people, not because they deserved them. They were withdrawn from those who used them foolishly and transferred to a more faithful steward. *Ye ask, and receive not, because ye ask amiss, that ye may consume it upon your lust - James 4:3.*

In order to be a success God's way, remember these basic principles:

Yield to God - Every successful servant of God who was given material and spiritual blessings first demonstrated an acceptance of God's lordship.

Obey God - Those who are truly blessed by God have demonstrated a willingness to use their assets for God. Literally, the more they let God, the more God is able to glorify Himself through them. An unwavering dedication to God's way is the mark of a true steward. (2 Corinthians 10:5-6)

Be steadfast in God - One characteristic of a successful person is being able to persevere in the face of problems. God wants people who don't give up easily. If God's people give up easily when faced with difficulties, who will be a living testimony to the people who need strength? Nothing and nobody should be able to shake a true believer from doing God's will. (Esther 4:16; Acts 21:13).

God did not create you to be a failure. God designed you to be successful! He will combine your abilities with His plan to create a lifetime of successes. That's not to say your life won't have challenges or difficulties. What it does mean is that God will prepare you for those times and will be with you each step of the way. To be in God's game, you have to learn about God and His rules. Knowledge about God helps you understand His plan for you and will keep you on His track. Putting God in your lifetime planning is the way to score those little and big successes.

Chapter Ten

Finding Contentment

P oor money management can cause frustration and worry. Living by God's financial plan provides peace and freedom. This does not mean that you will be problem free. We are human and subject to making mistakes. But once you let God control your finances, His divine correction will bring this area back under control. God's Word tells us to learn to be content and dedicate ourselves to serving God. (Hebrews 12:1) Instead, we put ourselves in bondage by following the world's slogan that says bigger and more are better. God wants us to understand that money is a tool to use in accomplishing His plan through us.

Do things God's way. Have you ever been absolutely convinced you were going the right way? You head off in the direction you picked with confidence and energy. Pretty soon you realize that things don't look very familiar. In fact, you have no idea where you are. You get worried, and nervous, and you feel oddly alone. You trudge around until you're all worn out. If you had stopped and looked at God's map first, you wouldn't have gotten lost. When we follow God and do it His way, things become very clear. We know where we've been, we know what we're doing, and we know our destination. *Thy word is a lamp unto my feet, and a light unto my path - Psalm 109:105.* God wants to keep us on a safe and joyful path. We can help by doing things His way. Remember He created everything and He knows how it works.

Get your priorities in order. Many of us are discontented, not because we aren't doing well but because we think others seem to be doing better. *Let your conversation be without covetousness; and be content with such things as ye have: for he hath said, I will never leave thee, nor forsake thee - Hebrews 13:5.* Too often, we let the urgent things take priority over the important things. Virtually every get rich quick scheme is directed at those who have not established firm priorities. They imply that more money is the only way to glorify God and that it is a sign of failure not to have every desire met.

Establish a reasonable standard of living. Having a surplus doesn't mean that it's there for us to use as we want. *So is he that layeth up treasure for himself, and is not rich toward God - Luke 12:21.* It is important to develop a lifestyle based on conviction, not circumstances. *Seeing then that all these things shall be dissolved, what manner of persons ought ye to be in all holy conversation and godliness - 2 Peter 3:11.* Just having an abundance is not a sign of God's blessings. Satan can easily duplicate any worldly riches. God's riches are without sorrow and are for bringing others to salvation. A disciplined lifestyle, with an abundance, is a greater witness than the abundance could ever be.

Develop a thankful attitude. Whatever happened to being thankful for the things we have? Many of us can't seem to do that because we are too busy trying to accumulate more and more things. When Satan convinces us to compare ourselves to others, then he has successfully trapped us into becoming the mouse in the spinning wheel - we're moving but not getting anywhere. James 3:14-15 reads *But if ye have bitter envying and strife in your hearts, glory not, and lie not against the truth. This wisdom descendeth not from above, but is earthly; sensual, devilish.* The best defense against this attitude is to give praise to God for the things you have. Satan uses the accumulation of many things we don't need or use to create discontent and selfish ambition. Thankfulness is a state of mind, not an accumulation of assets. Until we can truly thank God for what we have and be willing to accept that as God's plan for our life, contentment will never be possible.

Reject a fearful spirit. A favorite tool of Satan is the question, "What if?" Too many people get trapped into accumulating more than what they need because they fear the "What if?" of retirement, disability, unemployment, economic collapse, and so on. Obviously, God wants us to consider these things and even plan for them - within reason. But when fear dictates to the point that giving to God's work is hindered, foolish risks are assumed, and worry becomes the norm rather than the exception, contentment is impossible. *For God hath not given us the spirit of fear; but of power, and of love, and of a sound mind - II Timothy 1:7.*

Learn to be patient. We live in a fast paced society that wants everything right away. Why wait and save for something when you can use credit and get it right now? Why wait and see what God's plan for your life will be when you can help Him out and start on your own plan right now?

When we don't get things fast enough, we become impatient with God. Impatience leads to unhappiness, and unhappiness leads to disobedience. *And they journeyed from Mount Hor by the way of the Red Sea, to compass the land of Edom: and the soul of the people was much discouraged because of the way. And the people spake against God, and against Moses, Wherefore have ye brought us up out of Egypt to die in the wilderness? For there is no bread, neither is there any water; and our soul loatheth this light bread - Numbers 21:4-5.* Just like the Israelites, we wonder what's taking God so long! Remember, God's time is not our time. Trust Him to give you the things you need when He knows you should have them. It's also wise to remember that anything worth having is worth waiting for.

PART II

FINANCIAL PLANNING - GOD'S WAY

Give instruction to a wise man, and he will be yet wiser:
teach a just man, and he will increase in learning.
Proverbs 9:9

Is there anyone who wants to be
a financially responsible steward?
Walk this way, please!

Chapter Eleven

Got a plan?

P lanning is an essential element in any financial program, but particularly so for the financially responsible steward. God is an orderly provider and expects the same attitude from us. The first step in planning is to develop a changed attitude. This requires more than an initial try at creating plans. You must see them in everyday decisions. Don't let a stumble on your financial journey turn into a roadblock. Press your way until you can develop the plan God wants you to have.

A plan can mean the foundation or ground level of something; or a plan can be defined as a method for achieving an end. In other words, a plan isn't wandering around with absolutely any idea where you're going. That's not a plan, that's a maze. However, before you start your plan, you must have a clear idea of where you want to be when it's finished. Your plan should outline different parts of your life and how they fit together, for example, your devotional time, church, work, and family. It helps you prepare for life, gets you where God wants you to be and keeps you on track while you're going there. It's using God's teaching (your Bible) as a blueprint.

Start by developing short-range plans. Short-range plans are those that occur daily. These may include paying monthly bills, saving for vacation, saving for emergencies, or even paying taxes. After you get a handle on short-range plans, start developing long-range plans. Long-range plans are fundamental to the future success of family goals. If they are made according to God's principles, the rewards will pass from parents to children. It's important that the whole family be made a part of God's sharing plan. Husbands and wives should discuss these principles with their children. These attitudes, learned early, will pay dividends in freedom from financial greed and worry.

Here are a few financial principles to help in preparing your family budget:

Know the importance of preparing a budget - When written plans and goals have been established, the family can clearly see a visible objective standard toward which to work. In the home that plan is called a budget (some people prefer the term spending plan). Developing a budget will allow you to see your financial condition. If you think I'm going to start out by saying that this will be easy, think again. Knowing your financial condition means taking an honest look at yourself and not denying that a problem exists. For most people, money defines who they are and if there is a problem, it is swept under the carpet so that no one will know. THEY don't have to know but YOU do! It's time to stop fooling yourself. If you need help, admit it, and seek help for it. As you are willing to change the bad habits for good ones, God will step in and make those changes possible.

Give God's portion first - Pay your tithes and offerings. Period. No ifs, ands, or buts.

Set your own goals - Those who allow others to establish their plans and goals are going to be unhappy. Unfortunately, that is often the case. Some people are made to feel guilty because of their less worldly goals and allow others to change the course. Remember, God has a plan for your life. Your neighbor does not.

Seek God's plan for living within the budget - Before purchasing, give God an opportunity to provide the item. Also, pray about every expenditure. That experience brings God directly into our lives and strengthens our faith so that we can trust Him in greater things.

Get out of debt - Debt isn't pleasant. It can prevent you from following your dreams, or following your hearts desire to serve God in some profound way. Debt has a unique ability to destroy wealth, damage relationships, and dispel joy when it ceases being a tool and becomes a noose with which we hang ourselves. In the Bible, borrowing and lending were not used as a way to finance life. It was used as a way to help the poor. The way debt is viewed today is the reverse of God's system. We want things NOW and hope we can pay for them later.

There is nothing wrong with spending and enjoying money as long as we are following God's financial principles. The earlier we learn this, the easier our financial journey is going to be. We can be righteous in the way we handle money matters. Everything in our lives must have God as its foundation to work properly. When we see ourselves traveling on the wrong path, let's reach for God's help first. We'll breathe easier when we do.

Seek good Christian counsel - To get help you must be willing to ask for it. Many Christians are willing to help others but will never ask for help themselves. That is ego. No one is without difficulties, and therefore each of us needs some counsel and advice. I strongly encourage all pastors to develop, in their church, a financial library and also a financial directory of people that can be of help in times of financial crisis.

Have one bookkeeper - Both the husband AND the wife need to know about ALL savings, checking, and investments. However, having one bookkeeper means less confusion in handling money. The person who handles the money needs to maintain good records and keep the spouse informed in all matters of spending and saving.

I'm going to let you in on a little secret: Money is the number one reason many marriages end in divorce. Secret accounts on the side and lack of communication about money matters allow Satan the opportunity to use you in his quest to steal, kill and destroy. We need more husband/wife teams to help keep Satan in his place. Communication is the key and unity is the bond that will help to make money management in the home a less stressful process.

Prepare a financial statement - It's a very good idea to prepare a financial statement. A financial statement is a snapshot of your financial condition at a specific point in time. It is a statement of how much you are worth in dollars after you add up your assets (cash, checking and savings accounts, money market accounts, stocks, bonds, real estates, automobiles, personal property, etc.) and deduct your liabilities or debts (mortgages, credit card debt, personal loans, auto loans, etc.). Don't get discouraged if your net worth is a negative number! You need to know where you are financially. Remember, this is all about taking the blinders off and becoming a financially responsible steward. After you get over the shock, start preparing a plan to put you in a better financial position. Preparing a statement periodically helps you keep track of your progress.

FAMILY FINANCIAL STATEMENT
As of _____
(date)

🖊 ASSETS

Cash and Cash Equivalents:

Cash	$_____
Checking Accounts	$_____
Savings Accounts	$_____
Money Market Accounts	$_____

Investments:

Stocks	$_____
Bonds	$_____
Insurance	$_____
Mutual Funds	$_____

Other Assets:

Real Estate	$_____
Automobiles	$_____
Personal Property	$_____

TOTAL ASSETS $_____

🖊 LIABILITIES

Mortgages	$_____
Credit Card Debt	$_____
Personal Loans	$_____
Auto Loans	$_____
Student Loans	$_____

TOTAL LIABILITIES $_____

NET WORTH $_____
(total assets minus total liabilities)

Chapter Twelve

Balance Your Checkbook!

I know what you're thinking. Everyone knows how to keep and balance their checkbook! I'm afraid that's not true. The first time I conducted a seminar, a woman approached me and asked about the proper way to maintain a checking account. Learn to balance your checkbook because a financially responsible steward doesn't bounce checks. If it is hard to remember to write down the dollar amount in your register as you write a check, consider getting duplicate checks because each one would have its own carbon copy record. Also, be sure to write in the "FOR" section of the check the reason why you are writing the check.

If you don't know how to balance your checkbook, don't be afraid to ask your local bank to help. That's what you pay them for. These steps (and the worksheet that follows) can help if you can't make it to the bank.

✓Step 1
Assemble your checking account statement, canceled checks, your checkbook register or stubs, a checkbook balancing worksheet (most banks provide you with this and it is usually found on the back of your statement), pencil and eraser.

✓Step 2
Place canceled checks in numerical order. Look at the statement and compare the actual canceled check with the amount of the check as noted on the statement. Banks do make mistakes.

✓Step 3
Go through your check stubs or register and check off each check that has been enclosed with this statement. Any checks that you did not check off will be considered an outstanding check.

✓Step 4
Be sure to note any bank charges, such as cost of checks or service fees. Enter these into your check register and deduct these

amounts as though you had written a check for the amount.

✓Step 5

Note any automatic or direct withdrawals and be sure to deduct these amounts as though you had written a check. Also look for direct deposits and be sure these are recorded in your check register and added to your balance.

✓Step 6

Make sure you have entered every automatic teller machine (ATM) withdrawal and debit transaction, if you have a debit card, as a deduction in your register.

✓Step 7

Now you are ready to enter all outstanding amounts on your worksheet and balance the checkbook. Did you balance? If not, did you add or subtract correctly? Most important of all: any errors that you find need to be resolved as soon as possible.

WORKSHEET
Balancing Checkbook for Month of _____

Checks Outstanding		Deposits Outstanding	
Check #	Amount	Date	Amount
_____	_____	_____	_____
_____	_____	_____	_____
_____	_____	_____	_____
_____	_____	_____	_____
Total	$_____	Total	$_____

Statement Ending Balance: $_____

Add Deposits Not Credited: $_____

Deduct Outstanding Checks: $_____

Reconciled Statement Balance: $_____

Checkbook Balance: $_____

Statement Balance and Checkbook Balance must agree!

Chapter Thirteen

Develop a Spending Plan

S top living in denial. It's time to start being accountable for what you spend and how you spend it. Whatever your fears, please don't underestimate the value and importance of recording your spending. Knowing the truth really will set you free!

Start by tracking your spending for thirty days on a week by week basis. This is simply a written account of money spent during a specific day. Writing it down is the only way to find out where all the money goes. Get yourself a little notebook and each day start with a fresh page and put the current date on top. For every thing you spend, write it down and keep receipts even if you only purchase a can of soda. That's it. One page per day, every day. No time off. No totals (for now). In the case of a partnership, both you and your spouse should keep a daily spending record even if one spouse handles very little of the family income. Remember this is not an exercise to spy on each other, but simply an effort to determine where the money goes. The fringe benefits of this activity will surprise you. If you are true to yourself and diligently write down every dollar, dime, or penny you spend, your spending habits are going to change dramatically simply because of the commitment to record. Knowing you'll have to write it down makes you think twice before you drop a twenty-dollar bill on something you might otherwise have purchased in a moment of impulsiveness.

Now it is time to develop expense categories that are unique to you and your family. Start with the general categories like telephone, credit card payments, groceries, rent, clothing, savings, etc. and go from there. At the end of week one, gather the seven days' spending records, putting amounts in the various categories you compiled. This will give you a very good idea as to what you spend in a week.

At the end of the four-week period, you will now be able to look at your spending for a month. At this point you need to determine your average monthly income. Use the formulas below if needed. Add up total monthly expenses and deduct this amount from your monthly income. Will this be an eye opener for you! Doesn't it make a difference seeing the actual figures on paper? Go ahead, gasp a little. Maybe this will make you see that it is time to change your habits. Now that you see the problems, you have the power to change them.

Using a record keeping book, plan your spending by deciding category by category how much you want to spend. As purchases are made, write down how much was spent in the appropriate category. At the end of the month, total each category. Compare what you spent with what you planned to spend. If your spending was quite different from your plan, find out why so you can revise and improve the plan. Do not expect to have a perfect spending plan the first time you set up one. The idea is to keep working and reworking the plan until it suits your family.

Here is a simple formula for determining your average monthly income:
If you are paid weekly - Multiply your income by 4.333
If you are paid biweekly - Multiply your income by 2.167
If you are paid semimonthly - Multiply your income by 2
If you are paid quarterly - Divide your quarterly income by 3
If you are paid annually - Divide your yearly income by 12

FAMILY SPENDING AND SAVINGS PLAN

Category	Wk 1	Wk 2	Wk 3	Wk 4	Total Spent	Spending Goal
Tithes	___	___	___	___	___	___
Taxes	___	___	___	___	___	___
Saving	___	___	___	___	___	___
Giving	___	___	___	___	___	___
Housing	___	___	___	___	___	___
Food	___	___	___	___	___	___
Utilities	___	___	___	___	___	___
Telephone	___	___	___	___	___	___
Cable	___	___	___	___	___	___
Clothing	___	___	___	___	___	___
Insurance: Life/Health	___	___	___	___	___	___
Medical	___	___	___	___	___	___
Automobile: Gas/Insurance Loans/Repairs	___	___	___	___	___	___
Gifts	___	___	___	___	___	___
Recreation	___	___	___	___	___	___
Credit Card	___	___	___	___	___	___
Other Loans	___	___	___	___	___	___
Miscellaneous	___	___	___	___	___	___
TOTALS	___	___	___	___	___	___

Monthly Income $_____
Less Amount Spent for the Month $_____
Amount Remaining $_____

✎ Work at your plan until the amount remaining balance becomes a positive number! If this is a positive number for you and your family, let me extend my congratulations! Now seek God for how your surplus should be spent.

Chapter Fourteen

Reduce or Eliminate the Use of Credit

Y ou've seen the commercials. The people in the commercial are having fun! They dress right, laugh a lot, go where you've only dreamed of, and have the ticket to get there. That ticket is a credit card. How exciting, how now, how happening! Well, technically speaking, the credit card is an incredible advancement in the world of finances. You can be in a store in Miami, St. Louis or Seattle and if you have a credit card, you don't need cash. Just hand over the card, sign your name, and collect your merchandise. Thirty or forty days later, you'll receive a printed statement itemizing your shopping spree. All you have to do is pay the bill. What could be easier?

Like many things in life, that fantasy ticket to fun has a hidden price. Credit cards can fool you into thinking they're just like money - but they aren't. When you use a credit card, you're borrowing money. Just like with any other institution that lets you borrow money, the credit card companies charge you for using their money. Their fee or interest rate is very high! It doesn't take a whole lot of credit card use before you have one steep loan with a very high interest payment that gets bigger every week you don't pay it back. The Bible cautions us, *The rich ruleth over the poor, and the borrower is servant to the lender - Proverbs 22:7.* Credit companies can demand payment in other forms like lawsuits, repossessing items, or taking money straight from your paychecks. Credit card debt can haunt you and damage your credit rating.

The problem begins with a tiny line on the statement: ***Minimum Payment Due.*** The number after those exhilarating words is awfully attractive - and a lot smaller than the number showing your total balance. In fact, it may be one of the most deliciously destructive traps ever devised. Once it catches you, it doesn't let go. Why? Most credit card accounts are compound interest loans in disguise. When you buy something with your credit card and don't pay the bill in full when it arrives, the issuer (lender) treats it as a loan and lets you pay it off monthly. If you do this a lot, you end up with a balance that can reach thousands of dollars.

The interest (the fee the lender charges you for the use of their money - also called finance charge) you owe for that month may be more than the minimum payment. What do lenders do with the unpaid interest? They add it to your balance! The next month, you're not only paying interest on what you borrowed, you're paying on the interest. What's more, you haven't even paid off much of the principal (the original amount borrowed). So you still owe all of it. You're making payments on your credit card, yet the balance is going up! But believe it or not, it gets even worse. If you are late with your payment, or go over your credit limit, you are charged a fee. You guessed it - they add that to the balance too. Now you're paying interest on everything! By the time you pay off your outrageous balance (if you ever do), you will have paid enough interest to buy two or ten of whatever you bought in the first place.

The heart of the credit card problem isn't the card or the system. It's how we use the system. If we use our money and budgeting smarts, credit cards are useful tools. Credit only turns into debt when we mismanage our finances. In fact, a good credit rating speaks for our responsibility, management skills, and ability to use money wisely. So, credit isn't the enemy people think. Poor money stewardship is giving credit a bad name.

ALERT! ALERT! College-bound high school seniors and college students are attractive targets for credit card issuers. Even if you have no established credit, lenders are eager to capture your loyalty - and your wallet. In fact, banks spend millions of dollars each year luring unwary students with special promotions: no-annual-fee cards, gold cards, frequent flyer miles, special discounts on new cars, and other incentives. Many students run into trouble within months of receiving their first credit card. If you should ever run out of control with plastic, the card won't be the one that needs to be tamed. It will be you and your buying habits. If you are not employed and money management is a problem, you do not need a credit card!

TIPS ON CREDIT CARD USE

◆ **Shop for a card with no annual fee.**
Why would you have a card that charged you a fee even if you didn't use the card?

◆ **Only use your credit card if you have the money in your budget.**
Yet another reason why having a spending plan is important.

◆ **Pay off your credit card bill in full each month!**
As a matter of fact, as soon as you receive the bill and you have the money, send the issuer a check. If you aren't sure of your balance, call the issuer.

◆ **Keep careful records of all your credit card transactions and reconcile your statements.**
Some credit card companies will put in charges that you didn't make and if you don't notice them, then you are paying extra.

◆ **If you let a balance roll over into the next month, stop there.**
Don't use your credit card again. It's surprising how many people forget that the way out of a hole is up, not down.

◆ **See to it that your payments arrive before the due date.**
If you miss it, you'll be hit with a huge late fee and interest on the account balance. If you know you're going to be late, call the creditor and tell them. Sometimes they'll cut you some slack - but only if they hear from you.

◆ If the credit card does not give a grace period, don't even bother applying.

Most credit cards give a grace period on purchases. The grace period is the difference between the date you first make a purchase and the date your payment is due. If you pay the full amount within that period, there is a grace period, or free ride, with no interest charge - usually 20 or 25 days after the statement is printed. That's a good thing. But this wonderful grace period applies only if you paid off last month's balance in full. On some cards, if you have an unpaid balance from the previous month (i.e., you still owe money on the card), you are charged interest on any new purchases from the moment you make them. No grace period. No free ride. And for many, there is no way out.

◆ Always try to find the card with the lowest fixed annual percentage rate.

The annual percentage rate or APR tells you the fee the lender will charge for the use of their money over a period of twelve months. A fixed rate means that the rate will not change. Any card that will charge a variable rate is not worth having. Who needs surprises?

◆ Always read the fine print.

Are there any hidden fees (such as application fees) that do not show up in the big print? The card companies know that most people only read the large lettering. Be a smart steward and get to the heart of the matter. Read everything! Knowledge is power!

◆ When all else fails, get rid of the card.

When it comes down to a battle of who's controlling whom, concede the battle, cut up and cancel the card. A wild credit card habit is a sign that your budget and money management skills aren't healthy. Get it right, right from the start, and you'll be all right later on. But if you mess up at the start, you'll be fighting your bad habits for years to come.

So there you have it. A wisely managed credit card can be a real help to your money management and financial future. Or it can be a debt-trap that ensnares and holds you captive for years to come. Blessing or curse: The choice is yours!

Chapter Fifteen

Know What's on Your Credit Report

E very year get a copy of your credit report from all three credit bureaus and examine the report carefully. Just because you have a clean record with one bureau doesn't guarantee a clean record with the other two. A fee is charged by each credit bureau to get a copy of your report, but not if you take advantage of the free opportunities to get your credit report such as: your report is inaccurate because of fraud, you're on welfare, or you're unemployed and plan to look for a job within 60 days. There also is no charge if a company has taken adverse action against you, such as denying your application for credit, insurance or employment, and you request your report within 60 days of receiving the notice of the adverse action. If you live in Colorado, Georgia, Massachusetts, Maryland, New Jersey or Vermont, you're automatically entitled to a free report each year from each credit bureau.

Experian
PO Box 2002
Allen, TX 75013
To order report or to report fraud: 888-397-3742
www.experian.com

Equifax
PO Box 740241
Atlanta, GA 30374-0241
To order report: 800-685-1111
To report fraud: 800-525-6285
www.equifax.com

TransUnion
PO Box 1000
Chester, PA 19022
To order report: 800-888-4213
To report fraud: 800-680-7289
www.transunion.com

SPECIAL NOTE: Equifax automatically allows one free credit report per year regardless of the state in which you reside. Call 888-853-5099 for details.

The reports - which can differ because each company accumulates information separately - contain your name, address, date of birth and Social Security number. They list loans and credit card accounts, with credit limits, outstanding balance and payment history (if you ever paid late) for each account. They also contain any bankruptcies, financial judgments or liens against you, and a list of who has asked for a copy of your credit report.

Each report also includes instructions, forms and phone numbers to correct errors. If you challenge an entry in your credit report, the agency must contact the creditor and respond to your complaint within 30 days.

If you have a questionable credit history, don't fall for a company that promises for a fee, to clean up your credit report. According to the Federal Trade Commission, no one can legally remove accurate and timely negative information from your credit report. Companies that make claims to clean up your credit history, or demand payment in advance, do nothing to improve your credit report; many simply vanish with your money.

SPECIAL ALERT!! - Identity theft is on the rise. If you find that you're a victim, visit the Federal Trade Commission website (ftc.gov) or call the hotline 877-IDTHEFT.

Chapter Sixteen

Start a Savings Plan

Part of keeping a good budget is developing a good savings plan. If you don't have one, start now. The deposits don't have to be huge. A few dollars here, a few dollars there will do. It may not seem like much at first but it does add up. The important thing to remember about a savings account is that it's for saving. When you save, it helps you prepare for God's future plans and your financial needs along the way. Saving is smart because it keeps you free from debt and free to choose where, when, and how you're going to spend the money you earn. It is up to you to decide where to keep this savings account (bank, credit union, insurance) but whatever you do, don't keep it in your purse or wallet. Let's not give Satan a chance to take away what God has blessed us to have. When it comes to finances, here's the bottom line: You can't keep it all, but you can't use it all either. The key is balance.

Start with a plan. First, commit yourself to a savings amount and make it mandatory just like paying your rent or telephone bill. The best way to make sure the money comes out? Automatic savings. With automatic savings (this is used in conjunction with the direct deposit program), the money is automatically withdrawn and deposited into savings before you ever see it. You won't miss what you don't see. Don't have a regular source of income? You aren't off the hook. There are other ways you can start savings. Save all your change in a jar or piggy bank, keep a money jar in the laundry room, give up expensive habits, save all refunds, hang onto windfalls (unexpected gifts of money, bonuses, awards, etc.), save reimbursements, and you can even sell some of your assets (we all know about yard sales!).

If you are able to join a credit union, please do so! For the highest earnings on savings and the lowest fees and rates on loans, consumers will get more for their buck at credit unions versus a bank. Owned and controlled by their members, credit unions have less overhead expense than most banks and their not-for-profit status exempts them from federal taxes. Be warned, having your money in a credit union requires good budgeting of funds simply because credit unions tend to be less convenient in location and hours of operation.

Chapter Seventeen

Using Wisdom When It Comes to Spending

S pending is taking what we have earned and trading it for something we need. There is a world out there full of things we can spend money on but we have to use wisdom. Spending is not the opposite of saving. Spending is the process of using our money, whereas saving is merely delayed spending. So what to do? If God has blessed you to have a surplus of money, you can spread that extra money by saving and spending wisely. God is pleased when we spend our money on worthy things. *That they do good, that they be rich in good works, ready to distribute, willing to communicate -* *I Timothy 6:18.* When we spend with a God-based plan, we are a light to the world by showing our community the Godly way of handling money. People will wonder why we aren't in debt. (I still have people look at me in wonder.) Then we can introduce them to our Financial Advisor. After all, God's office is open 24 hours a day, seven days a week!

Reality check! Most people don't have nearly as much skill at buying as the sellers have at selling. Sellers have their plan down pat; however, you can sharpen your skills by learning the marketing strategies. Don't get me wrong. I'm not saying in any way that the marketing strategies are wrong. If you owned your own business, you would use many of these same tactics to sell your goods or services. My point is that you need to know what these tactics are so that you can become a better consumer. The result will be that you'll have more money to do more things, and you'll take control of your finances, buying decisions, and values.

Huge Discounts. The most common selling gimmick is to play with prices. When a store advertises a certain product at a "50 percent discount," your first questions should be "What prices are they discounting?"

Manufacturers sell their products to a store and give a suggested retail price that will make the store a profit. Let's say the manufacturer suggests the stereo store sells its new CD players for $50. The store doesn't have to sell it for a $50. It can sell it for more, say $100. That's fifty dollars more than even the manufacturer said it was worth. When we shop, we should be aware that we could be paying more than we should. Even if the store lowers its already high price to, let's say $80, is that a discount? Sad to say, it isn't. The lesson here is to investigate the big signs that declare "On Sale!" or "Great Deal!" Unless you compare prices, you'll never really know.

Save! Store owners know that many people feel a little guilty when they spend money. And just about everyone feels good when they get a good deal. So they distract you from how much you're spending, and congratulate you on how much you're saving. This is where the "discount price" really comes in handy. The old price was $100; the new price is $75: "Save $25!" Let's set things straight. You're not saving anything. You're spending. You may be spending less, but you're still spending. The only time you are saving is when your money is in a savings account. When you see those red tags showing the amount of money you're saving, ignore them. Look at the price. That's what you're going to spend, and that's what counts in your budget.

Watch impulse buying. Impulse buying is buying something before you have a chance to really think about it. Many stores rely on it. The supermarket checkout stand is a great example. You know you shouldn't buy that candy bar; you are there to buy groceries. But that candy is practically jumping off the shelf. If you had time to think about it, you'd say, "No, I don't need it." But the checker is just about to total your purchases, so you throw it on the checkout counter and pay for it without thinking.

There are ways to help you avoid impulse buying. For instance, take only enough money for the things you need. If you are in a department store and feel pressured by the salesperson, walk away and get some air. Come back another day. Another plan would be to take a friend with you who is also managing his or her money properly. It helps to have a good shopping team that encourages each other's spending plan. Another trick is the "7 over 7" rule. Before you buy anything more than $7, you must wait seven days. If you still want it a week later, you can buy it.

What time is it? Timing is everything in shopping control. Do you really need it right now? Can you afford it right now? Is this the best time to buy? Plan for your spending by choosing when you go. Don't go grocery shopping on an empty stomach. Don't go shopping when you are way too tired and stressed out. When you are tired, you can't focus on smart comparison shopping. You will just buy something to get out of the store.

Avoid "Get-Rich-Quick" schemes. When something sounds too good to be true, it usually is. This does not mean that all good deals are bad. What you need to do, as a financially responsible steward, is to become an investigator. When you discover that a group or individual is into fraudulent practices, inform others so that they too, can avoid the trap.

The only person who is always as good as His word is Jesus Christ! Learn it! Memorize it! Never forget it!

Take a list. Before you go to any store, put together a list of the things you want. Develop an attitude that if the store doesn't have what you want, then it's okay to leave without making a purchase. Just because you're in the store doesn't mean that you have to buy something.

The "Image" Factor. Look past the appeal of looking good or cool if you buy a particular product. The advertisers present their products in ways that will appeal to us; and they are the masters of trend. From the billion-dollar soft drink commercials to the billion dollar shoe commercials, they make us stop, stare and, most important, buy. Go for quality. Make sure the product lives up to its advertiser's claim. What can that product really do for you?

Chapter Eighteen

What About Bankruptcy?

B ankruptcy is never an action to be taken lightly. It shouldn't even be in a Christian's vocabulary. The financial consequences and the damage to a reputation are long lasting for anyone, but especially a Christian. God's Word teaches that the way we handle our money is the clearest reflection of our spiritual value system. As representatives of Jesus Christ before the world, we are admonished to think ahead and consider the consequences of our actions. It is not wrong for a creditor to expect to recover the money he has lent in good faith, and the Bible is clear in its admonition to pay one's vows. Regardless of how it seems today, debt is not the norm and shouldn't be normal for God's people. So is it wrong to borrow? No. The law of borrowing given in Scripture is that it is a sin to borrow and not repay. *The wicked borroweth, and payeth not again: but the righteous showeth mercy, and giveth - Psalm 37:21.* The financially responsible steward only borrows if absolutely necessary and already has a plan in place to repay in the least time possible.

The problem with bankruptcy is that for most people it is a quick fix. No one wants to suffer the consequences of their actions. However you really need to consider what happens because your credit is destroyed and a bankruptcy claim stays on your record for ten years. Understand that bankruptcy is a legal remedy, not a scriptural remedy. Bankruptcy of itself is not wrong but using bankruptcy as an avenue to avoid paying what is rightly owed is wrong. As a responsible steward you have an obligation before God and man to do what is right.

So if you are in financial trouble and you really need help, what should you do? Here are some helpful steps to take:

➤ First of all, you've got to face reality and accept responsibility for your actions. Go to God and repent for not being a good steward, commit to getting out of debt and ask for His direction.

➤ Realize that even though you are in debt, you still have rights as a consumer and you don't have to accept harassing phone calls and bullying from creditors. Collectors are allowed to contact you only between 8am and 9pm. If calls are made any other time, or the calls made threaten your family, send a certified letter stating that you'll deal with the matter only by mail. If the calls at that point do not stop, contact the Attorney General's office in your area.

➤ Get outside help, if necessary, to start preparing a good budget plan and to talk with creditors about a repayment plan. Be prepared to give detail to the creditors on how you will pay and how long you anticipate it will take to completely pay off the debt. If there are financial counselors at your local church who can help you, start there. Consumer Counseling Credit Service is also a good place to go to help you get started. To find the CCCS office nearest you, call toll free 1-800-388-2227.

➤ Realize that getting out of debt will be harder than it was to get into. It may take several years to pay back a debt that only took one day to create.

➤ If (and this is a BIG "if") bankruptcy needs to be considered then there are two types you need to be aware of:

Chapter 13: permits an individual under court supervision and protection to develop and perform a plan to pay his or her debts in whole or in part over a three year period. You pay no interest or finance charge on most debts, the court determines the amount of your periodic payments and decides how much of your debts you are able to repay. Most plans call for repayment of all or almost all debts. In using this option, realize that once the court appointed percentage was repaid, the remaining portion will still need to be repaid. *A good name is rather to be chosen than great riches, and loving favour rather than silver and gold - Proverbs 22:1.*

Involuntary: permits an initiation of bankruptcy by your creditors who wish to attach all available assets and force an individual to liquidate to settle all debts. Once this happens, no more debt legally is owed to the creditors. You are not responsible for what other people do, but you are responsible to God for your actions. For a Christian, the obligation to repay according to the original terms still exists. *Withhold not good from them to whom it is due, when it is in the power of thine hand to do it - Proverbs 3:27.*

A FINAL WORD

Many people think that they're not old enough or maybe they think they are too old, not smart enough, not rich enough, or not "whatever" enough, to change their financial situation. So they sit around and wait for that special time when they think God will make all of their financial worries disappear. Guess what? God doesn't check for physical characteristics when looking at how you handle His money. He can use you right now to affect a financial change in your family, church, community and culture.

So what are you waiting for?

Get out your money,

... tithe ... give ...save ... spend wisely ...

and you know what else?

You guessed it.

Always Be mindful of Christ!

REFERENCES

Burkett, L. Allen & Lauree. <u>Money Matters for Teens</u>.
   Chicago, IL: Moody Press, 1997.

Burkett, Larry. <u>How to Manage Your Money</u>.
   Chicago, IL: Moody Press, 1991.

Burkett, Larry. <u>Using Your Money Wisely</u>.
   Chicago, IL: Moody Press, 1985.

Hunt, Mary. <u>The Financially Confident Woman</u>.
   Nashville, TN: Broadman & Holman Publishers, 1996.

McCann, Michael D. <u>God Owns -- I Manage</u>.
   Cincinnati, OH: Standard Publishing, 1990.

- -

ABOUT THE AUTHOR

Karen Tobias has walked in financial freedom in 1998. She is the founder and president of ABCs of Money Ministries, a ministry started in 1999 to share God's financial plan with all people, teaching everyone to always be mindful of Christ!

Karen is also the author of "**Breaking the Strongholds of Debt**," a cutting edge testament of her faithfulness to do God's Will. The reader is taken beyond the simple financial formulas to applying God's Word to their financial situation.

She is a graduate of Mississippi University for Women in Columbus, MS and as of this writing, resides in Tupelo, MS.

Breaking the Strongholds of Debt

by Karen Tobias

Do you have money worries? Have debts become the "Goliath" in your life? This book is designed to get your mind ready for the task at hand. For too long we have been held captive to the wrong thought patterns concerning our finances. Make up in your mind that God will be the head of your life AND your finances. It's time to break the strongholds of debt!

"Breaking the Strongholds of Debt" and
"The ABCs of Money: Always Be mindful of Christ!"
are available in any bookstore
or you can purchase online at **www.abcsofmoney.com**
Get your copy and give one as a gift today!

- -

ABCs of Money Ministries
P.O. Box 4122
Tupelo, MS 38803-4122
mail@abcsofmoney.com

www.abcsofmoney.com

ABCs of Money Ministries is a 501(c)3 Christian financial ministry designed to educate people on the basics of money and how God should play the ultimate role in our financial lives.

Sign up to receive the ABCs of Money Ministries quarterly newsletter electronically! Send us an email and type "subscribe" on the subject line. Otherwise, you may write to the above address and we will add your name and address to our mailing list. Seminars and workshops for your group or organization are available upon request.